FINDING

R.M. Lala is the author of ten books including two bestsellers—
*The Creation of Wealth*, and his biography of J.R.D. Tata, *Beyond the Last Blue Mountain*. In his varied career he has been editor, book publisher and Director of Sir Dorabji Tata Trust, Tata's premier charitable foundation, for eighteen years. His books have been translated into various languages, including Japanese.

# FINDING A PURPOSE IN LIFE

*26 People Who Inspired the World*

R.M. LALA

SKETCHES BY VIJAY MOHITE

HarperCollins *Publishers* India
*a joint venture with*

New Delhi

First published in India in 2009 by
HarperCollins *Publishers* India
*a joint venture with*
The India Today Group

Copyright © R.M. Lala 2009

ISBN: 978-81-7223-856-8

4 6 8 10 9 7 5 3

**HarperCollins *Publishers***
A-53, Sector 57, Noida 201301, India
77-85 Fulham Palace Road, London W6 8JB, United Kingdom
Hazelton Lanes, 55 Avenue Road, Suite 2900, Toronto, Ontario M5R 3L2
and 1995 Markham Road, Scarborough, Ontario M1B 5M8, Canada
25 Ryde Road, Pymble, Sydney, NSW 2073, Australia
31 View Road, Glenfield, Auckland 10, New Zealand
10 East 53rd Street, New York NY 10022, USA

Typeset in 12/15 Perpetua
InoSoft Systems

Printed and bound at
Thomson Press (India) Ltd.

Dedicated to my dear friend, Dr M.S. Swaminathan, who gave me the opportunity to deliver the *Hindu* Millennium Lecture on 'The Role of Purpose in Life', and to N. Ram, Editor-in-Chief of the *Hindu* Group of Papers, who suggested I do a book on the subject.

I am grateful to Yasmin Daruwalla for enthusiastically typing the first draft of the book and Villoo Karkaria for finalizing the manuscript for the press.

# CONTENTS

CONTENTS

## PART III

## PART IV

## PART V

## PART VI

# PREFACE

There is a pilgrim soul in all of us, an inner searching that continues throughout our lives.

Lacking a purpose in life, despairing millions seek refuge in drugs and alcohol, in crime and other antisocial behaviour. They are the walking wounded of our world. They have no one to turn to. Those with money may lose themselves in unbridled consumerism or sex – 'the good life' – but deep within, the nagging feeling remains. Man wants to know his place in this bewildering world, a place where he can anchor his spirit, find a direction, and pursue a purpose beyond his own advancement. Those who find it, have a sparkle in their eyes even at eighty years of age; those who don't, look vacant-eyed even at forty.

Such was my state when I graduated from college at the age of nineteen. Although intellectually well furnished, I was spiritually starved. In my quiet moments, I would ask myself: 'Why am I in this world? Is there a God? What is the meaning of life?' Like many today, I found an immediate outlet in frenzied activity, handling more than one task at a time – in my case, journalism and publishing. But a career is not a purpose. A noble purpose is one that is deeply satisfying not only to your own self but also beneficial to others. Lucky are those whose career and purpose match. The rest of us have to find a purpose beyond our careers or within them.

## My Own Search

I had a Marxist teacher who, when I was fourteen, robbed me of what little faith I had. By sixteen, I was traversing the desert of atheism, arguing against the existence of God. That phase passed. Not long after, at the age of twenty-one, a personal crisis hit me. By then, I was open to believing in God. 'If there is a God,' I said to myself, 'let me have proof of it.'

I found a purpose in my life by trying to live by moral standards and through my discovery of God. In this book, I have elaborated on this. This impacted my career in writing as well. I made a transition from fierce criticism to writing which I felt would enable people to find something deeper and more satisfying in their lives. Many years later, in 1979, I met Mother Teresa. As I bid her goodbye and turned to leave, she said to me: 'Write something beautiful for God.' I found a purpose for writing.

When I completed my major biography of the pioneer aviator and illustrious industrialist J.R.D. Tata, *Beyond the Last Blue Mountain*, he asked me, 'What do you plan to write on next?' I replied spontaneously, 'I don't know, sir, but anything I write will attempt to make man better and nobler.'

## FEET OF THE DISCIPLES

In the course of a sabbatical in 1975-76, I attempted my first book, *In Search of Leadership*, which spoke about leaders ranging from Emperor Asoka and Julius Caesar to Mahatma Gandhi and Martin Luther King. I searched for the relationship between ends and means and how immoral means can even alter good ends. Moreover, I tried to provide insights into the conduct of men whose purpose went beyond self-satisfaction and fame. I had one advantage. As editor of *Himmat Weekly* for a decade, I had the opportunity to meet many interesting people who had found a purpose, Vinoba Bhave, for instance. In their book, *Power and Morality*, Pitirim Sorokin and Walter Lunden speak of Mahatma Gandhi, Vinoba Bhave, Abbe Pierre and Albert Schweitzer. Three of these have been covered in this book. Sorokin and Lunden write that the influence of these men 'seems to be coming from a superabundance of the supreme energy of unselfish love, with which they are graced and which they indefatigably express in their thoughts, words and deeds. Their influence comes from the same source which made Jesus, Buddha and other apostles of Love, possibly the most influential individuals among all the leaders in human history.'

Elsewhere Sorokin writes

After all, Jesus, Buddha, Mahavira, Lao-tze or Francis of Assisi had neither arms, nor physical influence upon millions and for determining the historical destinies of nations and cultures. Nor to obtain their influence did they appeal to hate, envy, greed and other selfish lusts of human beings. Even their physical organism was not that of the heavyweight champion. And yet, together with a handful of their followers, they reshaped the minds and behaviour of untold millions, transformed cultures and social institutions, and decisively conditioned the course of history. None of the greatest conquerors and revolutionary leaders can even remotely compete with these apostles of Love in the magnitude and durability of the change brought about by their activities.

While writing some books on the House of Tatas, I studied the evolution of the personality of its founder, Jamsetji Tata, from an ambitious businessman to one who had made the advancement of the nation his business. To this purpose he gave himself and a good part of his wealth. At the time of my writing, there was a scandal in India involving the printing and selling of fake government stamp papers, robbing the exchequer of Rs. 30,000 crores or more. The contrast was striking.

At that time, I was invited to give the *Hindu* Millennium lecture in Chennai. Asked to choose my subject, I decided to speak on 'The Role of Purpose in Life'. A few months later, N. Ram, editor-in-chief of the Hindu group of newspapers, suggested, 'Why don't you write a book on this theme? It is a very important subject.'

This book is not meant to be the final word on the subject. Rather, it aims to stimulate the reader to think out his or her purpose in life.

I have divided the book into six sections. The first deals with three personalities who have shown the power of purpose, Mahatma Gandhi, Abraham Lincoln and Albert Schweitzer. The second considers the difference between ambition and purpose, career and purpose, and instinctive and acquired purpose. The third section deals with the main avenue for a noble purpose, namely, compassion, and how the compassionate work of distinguished individuals has affected the lives of those around them. It includes the purposeful leadership demonstrated by Martin Luther King in America, and Nelson Mandela and Desmond Tutu in South Africa. In both these instances the course of history was altered and bloodshed prevented. The next section looks on purpose that continues from father to son. The leadership of India's former President, Dr A.P.J. Abdul Kalam, his concern for his country and its development, reflected in his engagement with the youth and his vision for a developed India, is considered in the fifth segment. Finally, I deal with the pathways to finding a purpose, and the impediments that one may have to reckon with in the process.

I remember speaking on 'The Role of Purpose in Life' to a group in Pune. At the end of my address, quite a few people engaged me in a discussion. Among them was a middle-aged lady, somewhat short, stocky and fair, whom I have been unable to forget. With a pleading voice she had asked me, 'How do I find a purpose in my life?' Two years later, when I started writing this book, I was able to track her down. This book is for her and so many like her. If it helps them to find something deeper in their lives, I shall be more than gratified.

**R.M. Lala**

Man has a great need to know whether it is worthwhile to be born, to live, to struggle, to suffer and to die — and whether it is worthwhile to commit oneself to some ideal superior to material and contingent interests — whether there is a 'why' that justifies his earthly existence... This, then, is the essential problem. Giving a meaning to a human being, to his choices, to his life, to his journey.

— Pope John Paul II, 1979, Castel Gandolfo

# PART I

# 1

## GANDHI'S PRIME PURPOSE

It is not what happens to you in life that matters; what matters is how you react to it. If any man had reason to be bitter, it was Mahatma Gandhi. Mahatma Gandhi had gone to South Africa as a twenty-three-year-old barrister on a legal assignment. In 1894, he fell victim to the discriminatory policy of apartheid in South Africa. Despite having a valid first-class ticket he was thrown out of a train compartment along with his baggage.

This insult was soon followed by another. He was asked to sit at the foot of a stagecoach. When he refused, the leader of the stagecoach thrashed Gandhi's ears and seizing his arm tried to force him down. Gandhi clung to the brass rails of the coach, determined to hold on to them even at the risk of breaking his wrist bones. At this point some of the passengers spoke up for Gandhi: 'Let him alone, don't beat him, he is right, let him come [inside the coach] and sit with us.' The man let go of Gandhi's arm.

In the face of such injustice, an embittered Gandhi could have come back to India. Instead, he thought of preaching non-violent resistance to Indians in South Africa to fight the system. When he met an Indian friend not long after, he asked to meet

3

Indians (mostly businessmen) in that town to organize them to stand up for their rights.

The Mahatma's grandson, Rajmohan Gandhi, writes in his book *Mohandas: A True Story of a Man, His People and an Empire,*

> Returning to India entered his mind but was rejected as a cowardly option. He would stay and fight, and for more than his personal rights, for a shapeless spectre had assaulted a belief deep inside of him—the insight, nurtured from childhood and confirmed by his three years in England, that all human beings, creations of the same God, were of equal value.

Gandhi realized he was fighting not an individual but the arrogance of power combined with the arrogance of race. 'Emerging from the depths of his soul, young Gandhi's decision to stay and fight was both political and spiritual. The two impulses had fused and spoken to him as one.' The experiences that could have soured him and made him revengeful became a launching pad for a purposeful life.

The struggle he waged in South Africa was historic. General Jan Christiaan Smuts, then colonial secretary and later prime minister of South Africa, and a staunch opponent of Gandhi, said: 'He was a very difficult opponent to fight with.' When Gandhi came out of a prison term in South Africa he presented General Smuts with a pair of sandals that he had himself made in prison!

On returning to India in 1915 he toured the country for a year and within seven years was the unquestioned leader of India's struggle for freedom from the British. The causes Gandhi

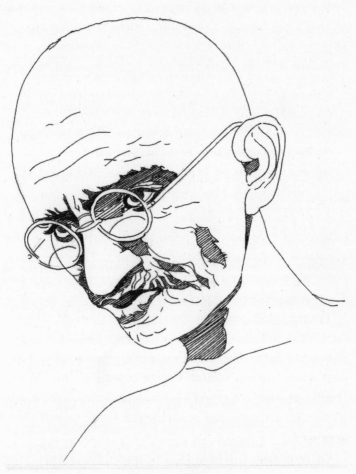

MAHATMA GANDHI

espoused were legion—from developing spinning and village industries, to the upliftment of untouchables, and communal harmony. These myriad purposes all fitted under the umbrella of God's will for him. Ostensibly, Gandhi was devoted to all these issues, but a man with a vision of God is devoted not just to a cause or to any particular issue; he becomes a devotee of God himself.

Jawaharlal Nehru, in his *Discovery of India*, spelt out Gandhi's impact in these words:

> And so he set about to restore the spiritual unity of the people and to break the barrier between the small westernized group at the top and the masses, to discover the living elements in the old roots and to build upon them, to waken these masses out of their stupor and static condition and make them dynamic. In his single-track and yet many-sided nature the dominating impression that one gathered was his identification with the masses, a community of spirit with them, an amazing sense of unity with the dispossessed and poverty-stricken not only of India but of the world.
>
> These unhappy dispossessed millions haunted him and everything seemed to revolve round them ... his ambition, he said, was 'to wipe every tear from every eye'.

Nehru put his finger on the spot. Gandhi's ultimate purpose was, in his own words, 'to wipe every tear from every eye'.

A purpose as big as this has to be shared with others to convince them to go along with it. And one needs to accept the fact that not everyone might share one's convictions. Among Gandhi's great qualities was his ability to carry along people who disagreed with him on certain principles. Jayaprakash Narayan, one of the founders of the Congress Socialist Party. wrote:

> Gandhiji always gave us the respect due to freedom fighters, and by his voluntary deeds, and more so, by his love and affection, he strove to win us over. That was why whenever Gandhiji gave the call and led the struggle for Independence, we Congress Socialists were ready to follow him as loyal soldiers in spite of our reservations with regard to non-violence.

Mark the words 'respect', 'love and affection'. It is only a noble man in pursuit of a noble purpose who is able to evoke these virtues. For one such, the purpose is not something to be blindly pursued for the satisfaction of the ego. Often the purpose is so big that one cannot achieve it on one's own.

When Independence came to India along with the trauma of Partition, a part of India was celebrating freedom from colonial rule on the midnight of 14-15 August 1947. In Nehru's memorable words: 'At the midnight hour when the world sleeps, India awakens to life and freedom.' But, where was Gandhi then?

He was trying to save Hindu lives, calm the communal passions that had killed thousands in East Bengal. On his return to Delhi he was equally active in saving Muslim lives. Pained by the violence that had gripped the country, a few days prior to his assassination by a Hindu fanatic, he had told his secretary, Pyarelal, 'Don't you see I am mounted on a funeral pyre?'

The secret of Gandhi was his faith in a divine source from whom he drew sustenance. Earlier, Benjamin Franklin had tried to tap the same source. After the Constitutional Convention failed to write one word of the US Constitution in four weeks, Benjamin Franklin addressed George Washington: 'I have lived, Sir, a long time and the longer I live, the more convincing proofs I see of this truth, that God governs in the affairs of men.' He therefore moved that prayers be said every morning before the assembly met. From that moment, it is reported, progress began and they soon produced what Gladstone called 'the most remarkable work known to men in modern times to have been produced by the human intellect at a single stroke'.

# 2

## LINCOLN'S MISSION

In *Light from Many Lamps: A Treasury of Inspiration* (edited by Lillian Eichler Watson) there is a moving passage describing Lincoln's departure from his little town of Springfield in Illinois, for Washington, to take up the office of President of the United States. A small crowd had gathered to give him a warm send-off. Neither his wife nor his children accompanied him to the station as she had quarrelled with him that morning. It was a wet, rainy day, and as he spoke, before stepping onto the train, his cheeks were wet with rain—or was it tears? He looked tired and worn, but his voice was warm with affection:

> My friends, no one in my situation can appreciate my feeling of sadness at this parting ... Here I have lived a quarter of a century ... here my children were born and one is buried. I now leave not knowing when or whether ever I may return, with a task before me greater than that which rested upon Washington. Without the assistance of the Divine Being Who has ever attended him, I cannot succeed. With that assistance, I cannot fail.

Lincoln never returned to Springfield. The conduct of those who were closest to him must have pained him no end, but it impeded neither his train journey, nor the more important one as President. Perhaps his most memorable words were in the Gettysberg address, 'With malice to none, with goodwill to all.' A man with a purpose is an integrated personality and when the chips are down, he has to show what he stands for. Even in the White House, his wife was never very supportive, but Lincoln remained undeterred in his purpose.

Lincoln's aim was to preserve the Union of America and abolish slavery. This he thought he would achieve by initially providing compensation to the slave owners. But the Southerners seceded and he had to go to war. Then he issued his Proclamation of Emancipation of the Slave, saying, 'A nation cannot exist half slave and half free.' On another occasion he said:

I know there is a God and that He hates injustice and slavery. I see the storm coming and I know that His hand is in it. If He has a place and work for me, and I think He has, I believe I am ready. I am nothing, but truth is everything; I know I am right because I know that liberty is right.

When, towards the end of the war, his forces were winning over the Southern forces, a man came up to him and asked agitatedly, 'And now, Mr President, how are you going to treat the Southerners?' Lincoln replied: 'As if they never went to war.' Thus, it was his purpose that dominated, not his personal feelings or a desire for revenge. He remained true to his words: 'With malice to none, with goodwill to all.'

ABRAHAM LINCOLN

Another factor that strengthened his purpose was his faith. On the eve of the battle of the Bull Run, the first major land battle of the American Civil War, a colleague remembers passing by a door that was slightly ajar. He saw Abraham Lincoln kneeling at his bedside by candlelight, pleading to God to show him what he should do, saying that his own strength was not enough to serve his people. His purpose was sustained by his faith in a power higher than himself.

# 3

## ALBERT SCHWEITZER

Grant, O Father, that Thy loving kindness in causing
my own life to fall in pleasant places may not make
me less sensitive to the needs of others less privileged,
but rather more incline me to lay their burdens upon
my own heart.

*A DIARY OF PRIVATE PRAYER*, DR JOHN BAILLIE

The concert halls of the capital cities of Europe were
resounding with the music from an organ played by a big
man well over six feet tall, with a shock of rapidly graying
hair, and deep-set, kind, blue eyes. His bushy moustache
distinguished him. The same hands that were regaling the
affluent of Europe with a rendition of Bach would, a couple
of months later, hold the axe and chop wood to make frames
to build the hospital at Lambaréné (along the Congo river) or
gently operate upon an African patient. The man was Albert
Schweitzer. At twenty-nine, he had a distinguished career ahead
of him. Few people of his age had three doctorates—Doctor of
Philosophy, Doctor of Music, Doctor of Religion. On Sundays,

he would play the organ and the rest of the week, he would teach at the seminary.

Schweitzer led a happy, comfortable life in Alsace-Lorraine until one day a thought came to him that it was incomprehensible that he should lead such a happy life in Strasbourg, even as he saw so many people around him wrestle with suffering.

> Then one brilliant summer morning in 1896 I felt I must not accept this happiness as a matter of course but give something in return for it ... I settled it with myself before I got up that I would consider myself justified in living, till I was thirty, for science and art, in order to devote myself from that time forward to the service of humanity.

He was influenced by the words of Jesus that 'whoever shall save his life shall lose it and whoever shall lose his life for my sake will save it'. He knew not what avenue he would have to take. All he knew was that he could not endure the thought of anyone suffering. He could not accept for himself the privileges of life that were being denied to others. He lived in the closest communion with nature and reality. He had an abiding conviction of the sacredness of life everywhere.

One day his eyes fell on an advertisement: 'The Needs of the Congo Mission'. A small hospital needed a doctor. There was no medical help for hundreds of miles. The mission was pleading for help from those 'on whom the Master's eye rested' to offer themselves for this urgent work. Schweitzer wrote later, 'The article finished, I quietly began my work. My search was over.' He decided that he would serve the poor of Africa by becoming a doctor. It would mean seven more years of study and a hard unpredictable life.

His search was over, but not the battle that was to follow. To Schweitzer's surprise, his close friends and relatives opposed him and 'tormented me beyond measure'. They accused him of burying his talent. Some would accuse him of conceit. 'I felt as a real kindness the actions of persons who made no attempt to dig their fist into my heart but regarded me as a precocious young man, not quite right in his head and treated me, correspondingly, with affectionate mockery.'

When, with three doctorates behind him, he went to enrol as a medical student, the dean of the medical faculty, in Schweitzer's words, 'would have liked best to hand me over to his colleagues in the psychiatric department'. Schweitzer concluded that anyone who proposes to do good must not expect people to roll stones out of the way.

After seven years of study, he went to the mission whose advertisement he had seen, with little hope that they would pick him for a job. But they did. Before leaving for the job, he went to the mission's office in Paris and asked whether they would provide the medicine for the work he was going to undertake in the forests of Africa. 'What medicine?' they exclaimed, adding that he would have to find his own medicines and surgical instruments to take with him. The only way Schweitzer could raise money was through concerts. He raised the initial amount from his concerts, bought the necessary provisions and went to Africa.

The small hospital served people 500 miles up the river along which Lambaréné was situated. Patients had no other access to medical help; they came by boat to seek medical attention. On the banks of the river, sometimes one would see crocodiles, their mouths wide open, waiting for prey. Schweitzer has described his efforts to save a man who had been gored by the tusk of an elephant and another whose hand had been torn by the frightful teeth of a gorilla.

A man of enormous strength and energy, he not only attended to his patients, but also expanded the hospital building with his own hands. He wrote countless letters to his patrons in Europe describing his experiences in Africa. The only luxury that he had was a zinc-lined piano presented to him by the Bach Society of Paris for his contribution to music. In the equatorial forest of Africa, music and medicine harmonized. Norman Cousins, the American journalist who went on to win the Albert Schweitzer prize in 1990, was one of those who visited the hospital at Lambaréné. Cousins relates how one particularly warm and humid night, when he had stepped out for some cool air, he heard strains of music in the distance. Then, quite abruptly, the music stopped. Curious, Cousins walked by Schweitzer's window. Tired by the day's work, his head held in his hands, the doctor had slumped on the piano.

Every two years, without fail, he would visit the concert halls of Europe and raise funds for his hospital. He disliked being away from his work and wondered how his people were getting on back in Africa, but it was a task that had to be done. In between all this, he found time to write prolifically, both letters and books. His books include *Memoirs of Childhood and Youth, African Notebook, Out of My Life and Thought, The Mysticism of Paul the Apostle, In Quest of the Historical Jesus, The Decay and Restoration of Civilization* and *Civilization and Ethics*. He also wrote on the ethics of the reverence for life and his autobiography *At the Edge of a Primeval Forest*.

World recognition eventually came to him. One day, news trickled in that distant outpost in Africa that the Nobel Prize for Peace was to be awarded to Albert Schweitzer, for forty years of service in the remotest jungles of Africa.

# PART II

# 4

## AMBITION AND PURPOSE

Purpose is a stable and generalized intention to accomplish something both meaningful to the self and of consequence to the world beyond self.

*NOBLE PURPOSE*, WILLIAM DAMON

An ambition that gratifies only the self cannot be termed a 'purpose', although one may like to convince oneself that in the long run, when one's goal has been achieved, it is this ambition that will become one's purpose.

### ASOKA: MISSIONARY EMPEROR

Emperor Asoka wanted to bring all of India under his rule. But at the battle of Kalinga, he was moved by the sight of the massacre that his ambition had caused. He saw people crying out in agony, horses writhing in pain, giant elephants felled to the ground. All because of his ambition.

Instantly, or perhaps in the days that followed, a conviction grew in him to abandon the path he had travelled on and take a nobler one. The capital of his empire was Pataliputra, just outside modern Patna. Not far from Patna is Gaya, where, under the Bodhi tree, the Buddha had received enlightenment. The Eight-Fold Path of the Buddha and his message of peace and compassion stirred Asoka. He decided to follow that way. In doing so, he left a permanent imprint on history.

Asoka sent his son to Ceylon (now Sri Lanka) as a missionary, and others to the Far East. A ruthless ambition had changed into a noble purpose, imbued with the desire to do good and to spread the message of compassion. Today, if one travels to Japan and visits its ancient capital, Nara, there are three massive statues of the Buddha seated cross-legged on the ground. The ear opening of each of them is so large that a man can walk erect through it. As I was watching this wonder, a Japanese gentleman next to me said, 'You know, my wife reads the sutras [holy words of Buddhist scriptures] every day.' When I met a Japanese publisher and told him about my book, *In Search of Leadership*, and that it had a chapter on compassion, he instantly said, 'I'll publish the book.' And he did.

Compassion is not just a feeling of pity. It connotes an urge or desire or strategy to help. That mankind in its frailty seldom pursues this path is not the fault of the Buddha or Asoka. However, people of all faiths in every country and generation have been inspired by it.

In his *Outline of the History of the World*, H.G. Wells wrote:

Amid the tens of thousands of names of monarchs that crowd the columns of history, their majesties, their graciousnesses, their serenities and the like, the name of Asoka shines there— shines almost alone—a star. From the Volga to Japan, his name is still honoured ... More living men cherish his memory today than ever heard of Constantine or Charlemagne.

## JAMSETJI TATA: THE VISIONARY

A noble purpose, as stated earlier, gives meaning to one's own life and is of benefit to others. This understanding dawned on me while researching and writing on the life of Jamsetji Tata. What gave one man, living in a subjugated country, the vision to place it at the forefront of the community of nations, of giving India not only the resources of steel and hydroelectric energy, but also a university of research as he envisaged of which even England had no equivalent at the time?

Jamsetji Tata backed his proposal for a university by offering to Lord Reay, the governor of Bombay, in 1896, fourteen of his buildings and four landed properties in Bombay. The income from these would be utilized to establish a university which would provide scientific and technological training to the younger generation. In his moving words to Lord Reay he said:

Blessed with the mercy of providence with more than a fair share of the world's goods and persuaded that I owe much of the success in life to an unusual combination of favourable circumstances I have felt it incumbent and due on myself to provide a continuous atmosphere of such circumstances for my less fortunate countrymen.

Jamsetji made it a point that his name should not be associated with the university. He also took the trouble of sending an educationist to Europe and America to devise an effective model of education for India. The Johns Hopkins University in Baltimore was recommended as the model.

The day after Lord Curzon landed in India as viceroy, the proposal was put to him by a committee of distinguished people of whom Jamsetji was just one. Although Lord Curzon's response was not encouraging at all, Tata pursued his goal undeterred. The university—which he envisaged as providing the intellectual infrastructure for the future of India—and steel and hydroelectric energy, which would provide the physical infrastructure, were the three purposes he pursued in his lifetime with vigour and determination. When he died in 1904, none of his three dreams had fructified. The only dream of his he lived to see was the Taj Palace Hotel in Bombay, a grand monument that still attracts the world to the city he loved.

But he left his benefaction for the university untouched and so inspired his colleagues and sons that they ensured that his three great dreams were realized. After Jamsetji's death, the Indian Institute of Science in Bangalore emerged as the fountainhead of scientific manpower, and many of India's national laboratories, like the National Aeronautical Laboratory, were born at the Institute.

He loved his country and felt deeply for the poor. A contemporary newspaper said of him that 'the advancement of India and its myriad people was with him an abiding passion'. The purpose he pursued became a passion. A chief justice of Bombay, Sir Lawrence Jenkins, said of him that he loved India

JAMSETJI TATA

'with a love that knew no bounds'. The point is not just having an idea but the willingness to give of yourself to it.

From Jamsetji Tata one learns that once a purpose is found one should focus on one's own course and not get involved in what others may or may not do. A young Englishman who used to go on long drives in the carriage most evenings in Nagpur, said of him that when you were with Mr Tata 'he talked of schemes and schemes and schemes. Never once did I find him impatient and intolerant or critical of another's shortcomings.' The last four words are important. Criticism undercuts creativity. Even while dealing with the most critical of people, Jamsetji would say, 'Well, well, there must be some good somewhere in the man.'

When Jamsetji saw the poverty of the farmers in the south Indian state of Mysore he asked himself how they could be helped. The only asset they had were mulberry trees. So he invited, at his own expense, two Japanese experts to start a school that would provide training in silk, right from the cocoon stage to the manufacturing stage. This not only revived the ancient silk industry of the state but also brought people from as far as Ceylon and north India to study there. Jamsetji requested the Salvation Army to run the centre. Once the centre came to life the government also joined in the effort. In a letter written in 1912, Booth Tucker of the Salvation Army says: 'The impetus given to the silk industry can hardly be overestimated ... The name of the man who brought the enterprise will be held in grateful remembrance.'

All of us cannot be an Asoka and Jamsetji Tata, but in our own way, by listening to the voice deep within us, we can discover our calling. Each one can discover it in his or her distinctive way.

## LORD JOHN HUNT: CONQUERING AMBITION

Sir John Hunt (later Lord Hunt) who led the first successful expedition to Mt. Everest kindly invited me to lunch in the House of Lords. I asked him, 'Even if Hillary and Tenzing were the first to reach the top, were you not tempted to be the third man on Mt. Everest?' He replied that the weather was good and he could have. In fact, it was planned that he and Wilfred Noyes were to be the next if the earlier couple failed. But, he added, 'We had always seen it as an integrated venture. It mattered tremendously that someone should go to the top—not who. It is not getting to the top of Everest that matters in life. It is how and why you get there. And sometimes it is better not to get to the top of a mountain at all. The victor on the mountain is the man who can conquer his own ambition, if need be.'

# 5

## Career and Purpose

A career need not be confused with purpose. One's attitude to one's career can turn it into a noble purpose. Say, two young men join a medical college to pursue a medical career. The object of one is to make money; of the other to alleviate the suffering of humanity. For the latter, his career was invested with a purpose, that of serving mankind without just making money for personal gain.

### Ratan N. Tata: Sacrificing for a Purpose

The man who dreamt of and made the cheapest car in the world was driven to school in a Rolls Royce.

Ratan Naval Tata went to Cathedral School and then to Cornell University to study architecture. After his education, he lived comfortably pursuing architecture in Los Angeles, looking forward to his future in America. However, there was one person back in India he was most fond of – his grandmother – and when she asked him to return to India, he obeyed her call.

He joined Tatas and was posted as a trainee in two of the largest Tata companies in Jamshedpur – Tata Steel and TELCO (now Tata

RATAN TATA

Motors). He proposed setting up a flying school in Jamshedpur and this brought him closer to J.R.D. Tata.

On his return to Bombay, he was asked to head a loss-making company – Nelco. At the lunch table one day, the other directors were severely critical of the company. JRD kept silent for a while and then he moved in, because he knew the future lay in electronics. Ratan says, 'He turned the discussion around. When you are fighting with your back to the wall, JRD would come and duel at your side.'

It was 1991 and the time came for JRD to step down. He proposed Ratan as successor. JRD told me, 'He will be more like me.' Ratan's first years as chairman of Tata Sons were the most difficult, but one after the other the satraps of the Tata empire fell in place and Ratan was free to take the group along the path that he had envisioned. It was the historic pathway of Jamsetji Tata and J.R.D. Tata.

When in 1979 I asked JRD why the growth of the Tata Group was less than that of other companies, he replied, 'I have often thought of it. If we had adopted some of the ways that other companies did, we would have been twice as big as we are today. But we would not have it any other way.'

When Ratan Tata came to power, he made it clear that if the companies in the group did not observe the Tata Code of Ethics, Tatas would exit from that company. One company wanted to go into films. Knowing it was no place for ethical business, Tatas made an exit from that company.

Ratan relates that one MD told him that you could not do without corruption in his particular field of business. Ratan would not yield. He says, 'As the MD left my room, I said to myself, "We are losing another good man."' To his surprise, six months later, the man returned cheerfully to report that he had practised the Tata way and found that his profits had improved.

What is often not realized is that there is a price to be paid for holding on to one's purpose. In Ratan Tata's case, the price was a comfortable family life. Once, a newspaper carried a report on three ladies he had in mind for marriage at different times – two Americans and one Parsi. I once took the liberty to ask him why he did not go ahead. Ratan replied, 'One would ask me, "Why are you going to Bangalore?", the other "Must you go to New York?" I cannot function that way.'

With this conversation in mind, I wrote to him on 24 March 2003, just as he was about to complete his twelve years as chairman of Tata Sons.

My Dear Ratan

Tomorrow you complete twelve years as chairman of Tata Sons. Working on the new edition of *The Creation of Wealth* has helped me to appreciate your contribution in greater depth than I had hitherto.

You have been able to carry this load – the way you have – by a sacrifice of the simple pleasures ordinary men enjoy. The family takes its toll in time and energy too!

While no man is indispensable I find it difficult to foresee one man carrying all you do...

The very next day he wrote a very moving letter which he has kindly given me permission to reproduce here.

BAKHTAVAR BUILDING, LOWER COLABA ROAD, MUMBAI 400 005, INDIA

March 25, 2003

Dear Russi,

I am deeply touched by the kind words you have expressed in your thoughtful letter of March 24.

In these twelve years, I have tried my best to continue on the track set by Jeh, who has been my mentor for so many years. The years have been tough, with all the problems and blame for anything that has gone wrong directed at me — often without reason! Nevertheless, they have been a great learning experience — learning about human nature, hypocracy, true friendship, and, above all, values and integrity. Yes, there has been considerable personal sacrifice and a high cost in terms of family life and family relations — which I deeply regret. However, everything is worthwhile if I succeed in transforming the group into a bigger, better and more customer-friendly organisation.

I am pleased you are feeling better and hope your American doctor is also satisfied with your reports. Please look after yourself.

With regards,

Ratan

32

# M.S. Subbulakshmi: The Voice Divine

At midnight on 14 August 1947, to usher in an independent India, two ladies were selected to sing India's national anthem. One was the young M.S. Subbulakshmi. She was also invited to sing at the United Nations. Jawaharlal Nehru once said, 'Who am I, a mere prime minister, before her who is the Queen of Song.' Subbulakshmi became famous as Meera in a film made by her husband, Sadashivan. Although she could have made millions of rupees for herself, she used her voice to promote causes about which she felt deeply.

I was privileged to spend three days with her, her husband and her accompanists at the Moral Rearmament Centre at Panchgani. As she sang I noticed the affection with which she regarded her accompanists, speaking to them through her eyes and her smile. It so happened that the accompanists had their room next to mine. One of them told me of the affection they received both from MS, as she was fondly known, and her husband. He said, 'Because they give sacrificially to charities, I like to work with them.' When she was leaving, I requested her to sign the Visitors' Book. Her celebrity status notwithstanding, she said: 'My husband should sign first.'

MS sang to bring her listeners closer to God. She once said:

> Any raga has the purpose of directing the minds of the listeners towards God and His manifestations ... it's nothing but the devotion we show to the Divinity that resides in us. Those who wish to take to the fine art of music must be good people.

M.S. Subbulakshmi

It may not be easy to be a good person. There is, however, a great advantage. There is no time bar to becoming good. There is no question of becoming a doctor, an engineer or a lawyer after a certain age, but there is no age limit for anyone to become a good person. In the mind of a good person, bhakti is an instinctive growth. God Himself makes His home in such a mind.

When she comes on stage, she settles down with her daughter and accompanists as they tune their instruments. Then the voice that has thrilled millions is heard. First, you marvel at her technical virtuosity. Thereafter you get absorbed emotionally even if you know nothing of Carnatic music. Gradually, you shed the pettiness in your life and around you and are lifted onto another plane. With her own devotion and charm, M.S. Subbulakshmi has achieved her purpose of bringing her audience closer to God.

## H.T. PAREKH: A DREAM FULFILLED AFTER FORTY YEARS

One day in 1994, I had just arrived in Bombay from an outstation trip when I received a phone call from H.T. Parekh, one of the most respected figures in the world of finance of his time, and my close colleague at the Centre for Advancement of Philanthropy. In a faint voice, he asked, 'Will you come and have lunch with me today?' Having just arrived, I would have excused myself had it been any other person, but not with H.T. Parekh. At eighty-five, H.T. Parekh had been quite unwell.

35

On an earlier occasion, when I had visited his house, I had asked him, 'What is your ailment?' He had replied, 'Loneliness.' He was devoted to his wife, but she had passed away twenty-four years earlier. To cope with his sorrow, he wrote two volumes of letters to her recalling their happy life together. That afternoon, at lunch, he was more subdued and quieter than ever before. Ten days later, he passed away.

Parekh studied at the London School of Economics in the 1930s, pursued a career in finance and went on to head one of the largest financial institutions of India, the Industrial Credit and Investment Corporation of India (ICICI). In 1976, at the age of sixty-five, he retired. A year later, at a time when most men, especially those loaded with honours like him, are expected to rest on their laurels and enjoy retirement, he started the Housing Development Finance Company (HDFC), the very first organization to make housing loans available to people in India.

I had asked him, over lunch, when he first thought of the idea. 'When I was in England at the London School of Economics,' he said. 'But that must be forty years ago!' I exclaimed. He nodded. He said he saw in England how people owned their own houses on mortgage, and he wanted Indians to enjoy the same facility, especially as housing was getting more and more scarce. For forty years, he quietly harboured his dream, launching it only after retirement.

It was a time when controls and licences were very strict in India's socialistic regime. Dr Manmohan Singh, who was then Secretary to the Government of India in the Ministry of Finance,

H.T. PAREKH

recalled to me Parekh's zest and enthusiasm for the project. Dr Singh said, 'It was an unknown adventure, practically the first of its kind in housing in India. No one knew whether it would click, but he had obtained promises of funds from abroad and he was enthusiastic.' They went on to become good friends when Dr Singh became Governor of the Reserve Bank of India. Such faith did he repose in H.T. Parekh that Dr Singh said, 'Whenever I had any doubts, I went to him. He was always so positive, always coming up with new ideas. He never stagnated.' Dr Singh could not give him much financial assistance, but he did give him his whole-hearted support by way of the goodwill and the permission of the government to start the first housing loan project in India. Over the next fifteen years, HDFC grew from strength to strength. Having thus realized his dream, he handed over the mantle to his nephew, Deepak Parekh.

Dreams need not die in the face of unfavourable circumstances. They may only be delayed. There is a right time for everything. At one such opportune moment, H.T. Parekh moved in with his vision which has benefited over a million Indians.

## DAVID CHANNER: THE SUBTLE CALL OF THE WILL

David Channer was a good friend of mine. At the end of World War II, as a young British officer, he was offered the post of aide-de-camp to Sir Claude Auchinlek, India's commander-in-chief. Channer had previously expressed interest in the idea of Moral Rearmament and the thought of building a new world appealed to him more than remaining in the army. He joined the Moral Rearmament full time.

Channer realized that his talent lay in photography and he was a tower of strength for the paper *Himmat Weekly*, which Rajmohan Gandhi and I edited from 1964 to 1975.

He was also a talented film-maker, who made many films in India. In 1986, he made *For the Love of Tomorrow* about the life of the French Resistance leader Irène Laure who, in the debris of post-war Europe, discovers a stronger force in forgiveness than in hatred. The apogee of Channer's achievements came in the last fifteen years of his life. In the killing fields of Cambodia, soaked with the blood of innocents, Channer was deeply moved by the story of a woman whose husband, a senior personality, had mysteriously disappeared. The woman wrote to Channer, asking him to make a film that would help forge a reconciliation in Cambodia, in the face of the UN-sponsored elections in 1993. Channer's interest in Buddhism also prompted him to make two other films introducing the West to the essence of Buddhist thought and culture.

In the aftermath of 9/11, Channer devoted himself to healing the divide between Islam and Christianity. He went to Nigeria, a nation with a predominantly Muslim population in the north and a largely Christian one in the south. There he made a film *The Pastor and the Imam*. He put the finishing touches to the film even as he was afflicted by cancer. The film was shown at the UN headquarters by his son and co-director Alan Channer, a few days after David Channer passed away.

I was witness to the forty years of the evolution of David, from a good photographer to a man of purpose, who sought to make his talent relevant to his times. I mentioned this to his wife Kristin who had left him free to travel the world with no demands on her husband. She said, 'If you let go, the purpose of your career opens up before you. It is the ego you have to let go.'

In the 1930s, a young man told Dr Frank Buchman, who had initiated Moral Rearmament, 'Frank, I am afraid to surrender my life to God.'

'What are you afraid of?' Buchman asked.

'I am afraid He may tell me to go as a missionary to China.'

'Don't be silly,' replied Buchman, 'he has a far higher opinion of the Chinese than to send you there!'

The point is, often, the ego creates its own impediments. In his book, *The Art of Remaking Man*, Paul Campbell articulates that the ego is wrapped round the will and the will is like an onion with concentric layers of pride, demand, fear, desire for recognition, fame, sex, security, and success. It is the human will that decides the direction of your life. David Channer had listened to the subtle call of the will.

## PETER HOWARD: A WRITER'S PURPOSE

Peter Howard was one of the highest paid journalists on Fleet Street before World War II, in what was then the largest selling newspaper in the world, the *Daily Express*. He used his pen to great effect, particularly when it came to pulling down politicians.

A lady connected with the work of the Moral Rearmament had a vision for him that one day he would be a man who will bring healing and a new life to other people. Eventually, the dream came true.

In the course of his life Peter Howard wrote ten plays on his own and some more in collaboration with others. And he gave British theatre a sound moral grounding in the 1960s when it was at its moral lowest. In a preface to one of his plays, *Mr Brown Comes Down the Hill*, he wrote: 'My plays are propaganda plays. I write them to give people a purpose. The purpose is clear. The aim is simple. It is to encourage men to accept the growth in character that is essential if civilization is to survive. It is to help all who want peace in the world to be ready to pay the price of peace in their own personalities. It is to enlist everybody everywhere in a revolution to remake the world.'

# 6

## INSTINCTIVE AND ACQUIRED PURPOSE

We need never be anxious about our mission. We need never perplex ourselves in the least in trying to know what God wants us to do, what place He wants us to fill. Our own duty is to do well the work of the present hour. There are some people who waste entire years wondering what God would have them do and expecting to have their life work pointed out to them. But this is not the Divine way. If you want to know God's plan for you, do God's Will each day; that is God's plan for you today. If He has a wider sphere, a larger place for you, He'll bring you to it at the right time, and that will be God's plan for you and your mission.

—J.R. MILLER, *IN GREEN PASTURES*

Purpose can either be acquired or be instinctive.

Sadhu Sant Singh was once travelling through the Himalayas when he saw a great forest fire. Almost everyone present was frantically trying to fight the fire, but he noticed a group of men standing and looking at a tree that was about to go up in flames. When he asked them what they were looking at, they pointed to a nest full of young birds. Above it, the mother bird was circling wildly in the air and calling out warnings to her young ones. There was nothing either she or the men could do to save the nest. Soon the flames started engulfing the branches. Just as the nest was about to catch fire, the men were amazed to see the mother bird's reaction. Instead of flying away from the flames, she darted down and settled on the nest, covering her little ones with her wings. The next moment, she and her nestlings were burnt to ashes. None of them could believe their eyes. Sadhu Sant Singh turned to those standing by and said: 'We have witnessed a truly marvellous thing. God created that bird with such love and devotion that she gave her life trying to protect her young. If her small heart was so full of love, how unfathomable must be the love of her Creator. That is the love that brought him down from heaven to become man. That is the love that made him suffer a painful death for our sake.'

A mother's love for her child is instinctive. It is noticeable even in animals. Among human beings, if one of six children is ailing, that child commands greater attention of the mother. I know a lady called Gladys who is a domestic cook. She works in two households to provide for her two children and her alcoholic husband. After her work, she returns home to do all her household chores. A few years ago, her daughter was suspected of a serious ailment. For seven years, she has escorted the child in and out of hospital. She speaks English and, like her sisters, could easily find a comfortable job in England, Africa or the Gulf. Instead, the survival of the sick child, Alvita, has

## GENERAL WILLIAM BOOTH: UNSHAKABLE

When an aged General Booth, founder of the Salvation Army, had to be admitted in a hospital, his eyes were failing fast. The doctor did not have the heart to tell the general that soon he would never see again. So he requested his son to inform his father.

The son went in and explained to his father what he did not expect to hear. He said, 'Father, the doctor says, you won't be able to see with your eyes.' The general replied, 'You mean, Brambel, that I will never see again?'

'I am afraid so, father.'

There was a pause.

Then the founder of the Salvation Army said to his son: 'Brambel, when I had eyesight, I served my God with all my strength. Now that I will have no eyesight, I will continue to serve Him just the same.'

GENERAL WILLIAM BOOTH

become the central purpose of her life and has kept her in India. 'I will never leave her,' she firmly says.

When a great movement like the Indian freedom struggle was on, many joined it. They acquired a purpose, namely, the independence of the nation. They gave their all for it. It was an important but not a lasting objective, and after Independence, many lost their idealism and drifted. Some faithfuls did continue because they saw the struggle as part of a larger struggle to lift the country out of its poverty and other problems.

God has a plan and a purpose for each one of us. The purpose may not be something grand, though we could well be led to something much bigger than what we may have imagined.

# PART III

# 7

## The Candle of Compassion

A disciple asked Buddha, 'What is the right action?'
The Buddha replied, 'Any action which originates
when your mind has compassion.'

—The Dhammapada

Pity is a noble feeling but a fleeting one. Compassion goes
beyond pity and wants to do something to set right the
situation. The path of compassion has led many to find a deeper
purpose in life.

### Vinoba Bhave: No Other Way Than Love

For twenty years, one man travelled all over India asking people
to donate land for landless labourers. Four-and-a-half million
acres were donated to this movement called 'bhoodan'. It
was more land than all the state governments of India could
command by legislation. The man who was able to persuade
people to part with their land was Vinoba Bhave.

It all began in the 1950s, when Vinoba Bhave visited the
hut of a low-caste Hindu in Andhra Pradesh and was shaken by

VINOBA BHAVE

the poverty of the family. He asked them what would alleviate their poverty and of the hundreds like them in the village. The unanimous reply was 'land'. That evening at his prayer meeting, he spoke of this experience. He appealed to the audience to donate voluntarily. As he spoke, his eyes fell on a rather well-dressed man. Soon, that same gentleman got up and asked, 'How much land do you require for this purpose?' Vinoba Bhave replied, 'One hundred acres.' The man said he would give it. That evening, the deed was signed and a movement that would bring tears of joy to thousands of landless farmers was born.

Vinoba Bhave used to say, 'I've come to rob you with love.' When I asked him if he would do anything differently were he to relive his life, he replied, 'No, I know no other way than love.'

## Dr M.S. Swaminathan: Feeding the Poor

Dr M.S. Swaminathan was a young man of eighteen when he read about the Bengal famine of 1943 in which three million people died. He said to himself, 'This should never happen again.' He had to make a career choice and he decided to study agriculture. He graduated from a college in Coimbatore in south India, and then went to Holland, Cambridge and America to study further. When offered a job in America he replied, 'I did not come to America to be of assistance to the Americans. I came here to learn, and assist my own country.'

He returned to India and became a professor at the Indian Agricultural Research Institute. He wanted to adapt the Indian

M.S. SWAMINATHAN

variety of the dwarf Mexican wheat discovered by Norman Borlaug for the Indian farmer. His superiors told him that the Indian farmer was very conservative and would not adopt new methods. Undeterred, he went straight to the agriculture minister who sanctioned the initial capital of Rs 500,000, a substantial amount in the 1960s. Despite the doomsayers, farmers in Punjab took to the experiment avidly and the Green Revolution was born.

But Swaminathan's mission did not end with that. Forty years later, he found that although there was food, there were still many people who were too poor to buy this food. He realized that the people were poor because they had no assets. One asset that can be acquired at a low cost is knowledge. In studies conducted at his own M.S. Swaminathan Research Foundation, he found that semi-literate women could operate computers competently. In turn, they could relay information like market prices to farmers and life-saving weather conditions to fishermen. He realized that here was a chance to make every village a knowledge centre. Knowledge is the most useful asset which the poor can acquire.

A purpose pursued with sincerity, can widen in scope with the passage of time. Driven by his purpose and his commitment, Swaminathan, even at eighty years plus, moves at a speed which would be the envy of a man of forty. Underlying this is his love for the farmers of India. When the Union agriculture minister asked him to head the National Commission on Agriculture, he said he would want it to be called a commission for the farmers of India because they are the people who grow food and are also the ones who are the most neglected.

Selflessness and a sense of service to others lead people to avenues that can give them fulfilment till the end of their lives.

## KIM BEAZLEY, SENIOR: IN TOUCH WITH THE GUIDING FORCE WITHIN

One's inner voice can be an instructive force in whatever field one may be engaged in. Kim Beazley, Senior, was a Labour member of the Australian parliament for twenty-eight years. He would often joke that he belonged to Her Majesty's permanent opposition in the Australian parliament. That is, till the day the Labour Party actually got elected to power and he became education minister. Just before his prime minister was to make his first broadcast to the nation, Beazley went up to him and said that the policy of Australia towards the Aborigines had to be changed. Under an earlier law, the Aborigines were prohibited from even learning in their own language. 'To deny education to a people in their own language is to treat them as a conquered people,' he said.

That evening, Prime Minister Gough Whitlam announced his new policy on air; the Aborigines would be taught in their own language and the government would help them in it. The injustice of one-and-a-half centuries was thus reversed in an instant; a change in the attitude of the white people was, however, more gradual. But it did happen in various endeavours for Aborigines.

KIM BEAZELY, SR

When as a young MP Kim Beazley was told about the absolute moral standards of honesty, purity, unselfishness and love, he burst out, 'It is absolute nonsense for a politician to even attempt it.' In spite of this he had the courage to try that path. Thus, the destiny of thousands of aboriginal citizens of Australia was affected by a man who chose to listen to his inner voice. It was Beazley's contact with the guiding force within him, something which resides in all of us, that gave direction to his life work.

## MOTHER TERESA: SERVING THE GOD IN MAN

'He created us for deeper things. There is some hand, some purpose behind our being.'

Mother Teresa was teaching at Loreto Convent, Calcutta, very comfortable with her students and studies; but every time she went to her room, she saw from her window the squalor of the Moti Jheel slum nearby. It made her spirit uneasy and in her many retreats, she sought an answer to this restlessness.

One day when she was on a train to Darjeeling, she heard the answer to her prayers. In her own words: 'I heard the call to give up all and follow Him into the slums, to serve Him amongst the poorest of the poor.' 'You accepted what the inner voice asked of you?' asked Malcolm Muggeridge, whose television film on Mother Teresa's life brought her work to the world's attention. 'I knew it was His will,' she replied. 'I had to follow Him. There was no doubt it was going to be His work but I waited for the decision of the Church.' Mother Teresa never doubted that calling.

MOTHER TERESA

Two years after this inner call, the Church's permission to devote herself to her conviction came through. Mother Teresa took a brief course in nursing in Patna and then returned to Calcutta. Here, she found people dying on the streets. The first person she picked up was a woman half-eaten by rats and ants. Mother Teresa nursed her but she died shortly. However, it marked the beginning of Mother Teresa's devoted pursuit of her calling.

When Father Le Joly S.J. hesitantly went to ask Mother if he could write about her, she encouraged him to do so. 'Tell them,' she told him, 'we are religious, not social workers, not nurses, not teachers … all we do, our prayer, our work, our suffering, is for Jesus … He gives me strength. I love him in the poor … Without Jesus, our life will be meaningless, incomprehensible…' She thumped her fist on the table and summed up, 'Father, tell them: "We do it for Jesus".' Father Le Joly took that as the title for his book, *We Do it for Jesus*.

There is no purpose more powerful than a religious one.

In 1979, I was privileged to meet her personally. I asked her, 'How does a person know for sure what his or her calling is?' She replied, 'Deep down in our heart, we know exactly what our calling is—if we are humble and sincere. God cannot deceive us. He created us to love and to be loved. He created us for deeper things. There is some hand, some purpose behind our being.' In the course of the interview she made an acutely insightful observation: 'If we judge people we have no time to love them.' As I was leaving, she gave me a purpose: 'Write something beautiful for God.'

## NELSON MANDELA AND DESMOND TUTU: LIBERATING THE OPPRESSOR AND THE OPPRESSED

Seven miles from the tip of South Africa is the infamous Robben Island prison, within whose walls Nelson Mandela was held prisoner for twenty-seven years. His offence was to organize the ANC (African National Congress) movement with fellow-Black Africans.

Most men would have been bitter or broken, but Mandela, a lawyer by profession, occupied himself in the useful task of educating his less fortunate fellow prisoners. Former president of India, Dr A.P.J. Abdul Kalam, who knows Mandela personally, puts it well: 'Mandela told his tormentors, "Any man or institution that tries to rob me of my dignity will lose." Mandela's major response to the indignities of the prison was a creative denial of victimhood, expressed most remarkably by a system of self-education, which earned the prison the appellation of "Island University".'

Mandela emerged from jail without bitterness. The task that faced him needed remarkable statesmanship. Talking about it, Mandela said:

> We emerged from a conflict that threatened to have this country rendered a piece of scorched earth and its cities flowing with streets of blood. We averted all that through a common commitment to a new observance of the human dignity of each other irrespective of racial, religious, cultural or other differences. Let us in this venture too remain true to that commitment to human dignity and equality of all.

While Mandela was still in prison in the 1980s, Archbishop Desmond Tutu, with his great moral authority, was doing his best for the Blacks. He did not want to battle the racism of white people by arousing racist reactions from the black people. Desmond Tutu stressed, 'We have to liberate not only the oppressed but the oppressors.' He urged his people not to be against white men. 'We want to share this country with you. Men must hold hands together.' He countered the physical might of the whites with the moral force of conscience. It was this moral uprightness that brought him world attention. The South African authorities could not dare to harm him, lest there be an uproar in the world. In 1984, his significant contribution to combating apartheid in South Africa was recognized with the Nobel Peace Prize.

A stage came when the black people turned against those within the community who they thought were informers to the white regime. Desmond Tutu called for a halt, but was unheeded by the mobs. Finally, in utter desperation, and at his 'worst moment', he threatened to pack his bags and leave his beloved land. Looking back, he says, 'I felt if I am doing God's Will, then He will perfect me.'

All the democratic forces of South Africa came together at the time when Mandela was in prison. Without consulting the other constituents, Tutu called for a march. When a woman leader from one of the constituencies went with a delegation to his house and politely asked him why he had acted unilaterally, the Bishop opened his eyes wide, bent closer to her and said, 'I had a message from God.' That was all.

NELSON MANDELA

When negotiations between the prime minister of South Africa and the coloured people were threatening to fall apart, Desmond Tutu came to the rescue. As the white South African President F.W. de Klerk put it, 'It was Bishop Tutu who came to the aid of both.'

A day came when it was announced that Nelson Mandela would be released. In sheer joy, Desmond Tutu literally jumped and danced with his people. At this point the real task for Mandela began; he had to win his supporters to non-violence and allay the fears of the whites. Mandela brought a visionary quality to his struggle and enlisted a moral integrity to unify a divided people. Soon thereafter, the country's first democratic elections were held.

But the bitter past could not be buried. Mandela and Tutu brought the oppressors and the oppressed face-to-face and established the Truth and Reconciliation Commission which reiterated that 'there is a need for understanding but not for vengeance, a need for reparation but not for retaliation'. The Commission comprised both blacks and whites. As soon as Bishop Tutu was appointed chairman of the Commission, he asked the secretariat of the Worldwide Anglican Commission to send nuns and monks of religious communities. He foresaw that the proceedings would be painful and that people would need regular intercession and counselling for the duration of the commission. 'Thus we knew that we were surrounded on a regular basis with fervent prayers of at least these groups of Christians,' he said, adding, 'as I grow older I am pleasantly

ARCHBISHOP DESMOND TUTU

surprised at how relevant theology has become, as I see it, to the whole of life.'

'The Truth,' it is said, 'will make you free.' For months on end, the Commission heard the declarations of the victims. The proceedings were televised for the public. It was a painful experience for the victims and there were moments when even the chairman could not control his tears. Sometimes he lowered his face and wept at the brutality of man to man. It was a deeply moving sight.

Tutu said: 'To forgive cleanses the self; to bear a grudge harms those who harbour it. The great good is communal harmony. Only together can we be prosperous.' His moral conviction, backed by the largeness of his heart ensured that the black people did not turn against the whites in revenge. Amnesty was granted to those who had honestly owned up to their wrongs and they had to confront those they had tortured or harmed. In his book, *No Future without Forgiveness*, Bishop Tutu says, 'As I listened to stories of the victims I marvelled at their magnanimity that after so much suffering, instead of lusting for revenge, they had this extraordinary willingness to forgive.'

Not one drop of blood of even one white man was shed despite decades of oppression and cruelty at their hands. It is a miracle of modern times. It was an astounding feat of purposeful leadership on the part of both Nelson Mandela and Desmond Tutu.

## MARTIN LUTHER KING: THE VOICE OF A PEOPLE

When Martin Luther King rose to prominence on the political map of United States in the early 1960s, the restlessness among the black people could have resulted in a bloodbath. Martin Luther King led his people to protest non-violently. He said, 'Christ furnished the spirit and motivation and Gandhi furnished the method.'

King was a pastor in Montgomery, Alabama, when in 1954 the black community decided to boycott segregated buses. King said, 'They came to see that it was ultimately honourable to walk the streets in dignity than ride the buses in humiliation.' And as the black people walked to work day after day a nation walked with them, black and white.

Despite severe personal pressures, Martin Luther King never succumbed to bitterness, preferring instead to channel his trials and tribulations to the betterment of his people. As he said

> I have been imprisoned in the Alabama and Georgia jails twelve times. My home has been bombed twice. A day seldom passes that my family and I are not the recipients of threats of death. I have been the victim of near-fatal stabbing. I must admit that at times I have felt that I could no longer bear such a heavy burden and have been tempted to retreat to a more quiet and serene life. But every time such temptation appeared, something came to strengthen and sustain my determination. As my sufferings mounted I soon realized that there were two ways in which I could respond to my situation, either to react with bitterness or seek to transform the suffering into a creative force. I decided to follow the latter course.

MARTIN LUTHER KING

As time went by, this conviction deepened. 'If every Negro in the United States turns to violence I would choose to be the one lone voice preaching this is the wrong way … Occasionally in life one develops a conviction so precious and meaningful that he will stand on it until the end. This is what I found in non-violence.'

Just as in India, Mahatma Gandhi's martyrdom resulted in a diminution of communal violence in 1948, so did Martin Luther's martyrdom in 1966 have an impact on the racial situation in America. Gradually the intellectual climate changed—not only of the black people but in the white community as well—and civil rights legislation came into operation with one enactment following another.

The climax came forty-two years after Martin Luther King's assassination: a black man was democratically elected president of the United States.

## Sudha and Narayana Murthy: A Shared Purpose

Sudha Murty was one of the first women in the mid-1970s to study computer science. After completing her course, she answered an advertisement by TELCO, the automobile giant, for the post of computer engineer. The application was rejected on the grounds that TELCO did not hire women. She was furious and promptly sent a postcard to the head of the Tata group of companies, J.R.D. Tata, saying that she had not expected this attitude from the Tatas.

She did not hear from JRD himself, but within a few days a letter came from TELCO asking her to come for an interview, for which they would pay the fare. When she joined TELCO, they apologized, explaining that they had rejected her application as there was no separate toilet for women! The postcard did the trick. Her speaking out against injustice, frankly and fearlessly, resulted in her gaining her rights. She was hired for the Pune office and later sent to Mumbai.

One evening, she was waiting for her husband to pick her up after work. It was seven in the evening and the foyer of the office building was deserted. Along came J.R.D. Tata. He looked at her and asked her what she was doing there. 'My husband is coming to pick me up,' she told him. 'I will wait with you till he comes,' he said. Such an important man was gracious enough to think of the safety and welfare of a young employee. And he didn't spare her husband. When Narayana Murthy arrived, he did not mince his words: 'Young man, never keep your wife waiting like this.'

When Narayana Murthy started his business, the seed capital was contributed by Sudha. Rupees 10,000 in those days would be worth about a lakh today. Nobody dreamt that this young company would become the second largest IT company in India, Infosys. All because Sudha Murty had faith in her husband's capabilities.

These are just some interesting snippets from the life of the woman acknowledged by all as the main person behind the success of Narayana Murthy. As the company grew and Infosys expanded its operation, the Murthys established the Infosys Foundation with Sudha Murty as its head. And she has indeed been a very active head. When I phoned her one summer day

Sudha Murty

in April, I was told that she was in Orissa to establish a hospital in an area that had no such facilities.

Infosys Foundation was established in 1996. It works in five states: Orissa, Maharashtra, Karnataka, Andhra Pradesh and Gujarat. The foundation works in the fields of education, hospitals, midday meals, amongst others. 'I enjoy interacting with people there, getting into their shoes. Poverty takes away their confidence and leaves them helpless. Those who only work in air-conditioned rooms do not understand that. When I visit them, I eat with them, interact with them, learn their language. My work itself is the reward,' she says. The word 'philanthropy' is derived from the Greek *fils-anthra-pi*, meaning 'love for fellowmen'. Sudha Murthy is a model of it.

Sudha Murty expresses herself not only through her philanthropic work but also through the articles which she writes. The series *How I Taught My Grandmother to Read* clearly shows her writing skills.

Asked about the motivating factor in her life, Sudha told me:

I have never been enamoured of money. My yardstick for respect was knowledge. Since my father was a professor, we had a lot of books in our house, but not a lot of money. One day I went to a wealthy family home at Malabar Hill, where food was served in silver thalis. But when I came home I mentioned to my husband that they were a poor family. 'What makes you say that?' he asked. 'They have a house at Malabar Hill.' I told him, 'Because there is not a single book in the house.' For many years, knowledge was the important yardstick of respect but I

NARAYANA MURTHY

realized that knowledge has to be used for the benefit of people below the poverty line. My purpose is betterment of society.

N.R. Narayana Murthy, the founder of Infosys, was born in Mysore to a schoolteacher father. He had four brothers and three sisters; all of them were very bright and topped their respective classes. Murthy qualified for a BTech course at an IIT but his father told him that with his salary of Rs 250 a month, he could not afford to spend Rs 100 on one child. Crestfallen, Murthy entered the local engineering college and graduated with a first class and distinction. That enabled him to win a scholarship to IIT, Kanpur.

In the 1960s, IIT Kanpur was abuzz with the enthusiasm generated by young American professors from eight US universities. It was set up with the assistance of American universities: MIT gifted the institute with an IBM 7044 computer. It was the beginning of Narayana Murthy's passion for information technology.

As a young student, his desire for social justice led him to accept Marxist ideas, and he considered himself a communist. However, a train journey to India from Europe, in the early 1970s, marked another turning point in his life. While on the train to Sofia, he was conversing with a French girl, not suspecting that the Bulgarian intelligence was keeping track. When the train pulled in at the station, he was arrested. For three days, he was incarcerated in the railway station room, which was a mere 10 feet by 10 feet. He was finally released because he came from a 'friendly country'.

Murthy now says, 'If they were like this to a friend, what would they be to a foe?' This drained his empathy for communism. 'I realized the importance of freedom of speech, of opinion, and the freedom to do things according to your conscience. I also became more convinced about the need to minimize the role of government and ideology in the lives of people. That also increased my faith in God.'

There is something fascinating about the life and personality of Narayana Murthy. The man, who twenty years ago requested his wife for Rs 10,000 to kickstart his dream company, is today a billionaire. Despite this, he has no servants at home and washes dishes and cleans the toilet himself. A role model for successful entrepreneurs, he has an ethical approach to life. Despite the prominence and prosperity he has achieved, he says his most prized possession is his 'conscience'. Through his work, he has found a high purpose in life. 'We believe in India,' he says, adding that a corporation identifies itself with society, and contributes to it and its policies. 'We have to add value to society.'

When I enquired about the scheme of giving sixty of his senior executives leave at half-pay for a year, he said, 'I have offered this scheme as a voluntary offering so that volunteers can give their services to society and also show their commitment by sacrificing half their salary. To enable them to choose the field of their voluntary work, we have created a platform where non-profit organizations can come and make a presentation at Infosys.' As the founder of Infosys, he headed the company actively for twenty-one years; at the age of fifty-two, he stepped down to become its chief mentor. When asked why he did it, he said, 'I wanted to give an opportunity to those with enthusiasm and energy.' I reminded him of what he had told me ten years ago: his desire that all those who worked for him become millionaires. He gave me the count in April 2009: 2000 of his staff are dollar millionaires, and 20,000 are rupee millionaires.

His purpose is to create a globally responsible company headquartered in India and accessible to the common man. He speaks of 'compassionate capitalism' and his belief that to achieve this, one needs to live a simple life. He continues to engage in the household chores. At the age of sixty-two he fractured his leg while cleaning the toilet because the tiles were slippery.

Narayana Murthy has kept himself busy—apart from being a member in the board of directors of many companies, he was also chairman of IIM, Ahmedabad, from 2002 to 2007. I asked him why he had taken that responsibility. He said he was very interested in higher education. He is on the board of Cornell University and is one of the overseas directors at the Wharton School of Business. 'If we are to excel in a competitive world, we have to give time to higher education. Compensation and power are looked upon as respectable factors in business. We need to create respect for a company.' He also speaks of creating a new index for judging a company, based on how well the company is liked, ranked, and contributes to society. If this comes about, the very rules by which companies run will become more humanitarian. Just another of Narayana Murthy's dreams for a better world.

## LEELA MULGAOKAR: CONCERN FOR SOCIETY

Leela Mulgaokar had everything that a lady could want: an eminent engineer for a husband, who was also managing director of TELCO (now Tata Motors Limited), a good house and money to spare. She could have easily spent her time in socializing and kitty parties but instead, she immersed herself in the problems of the less fortunate.

Once, a group of social workers went to a leper colony of Khopri near Mumbai. Those showing them around offered to teach whoever wanted to know how to dress the hand of a leper. None of the social workers stepped forward. Leela Mulgaokar did, and thus began her association with leprosy, which lasted for decades.

Following an accident involving her son, she was faced with the problem of unavailability of blood that her son needed. She managed to tide over the emergency but made it a point to ensure that others did not face the same problem. She started India's first voluntary blood bank at a government hospital in Bombay. It has flourished and brought out the best from several donors, including my friend, Rustom Davierwalla, who has donated blood over a hundred times.

Through the good offices of her husband, she got the Tatas to create a relief committee to address natural calamities like floods and earthquake. Companies in the Tata group would collect money and implement rehabilitation themselves. Leela had no ego and she included the wives of other officials and personnel and they worked as a team.

She usually lived with the people who were directly involved in the relief work, not all of whom were wives of senior officials. She shared their food and their lives, often under great inconvenience. On one occasion when she had separate accommodation she asked her co-workers where they were eating. She discovered that they were doing so at a local restaurant. She immediately arranged for her husband's company to send two cooks from Pune to prepare separate meals for people engaged in relief work. It was her individual care that drew people to work for others. She did it because it gave her satisfaction and a deeper meaning to her own life.

# PART IV

# 8

## FROM FATHER TO SON

A noble purpose being handed down from father to son is not uncommon.

Both Emperor Asoka and Jamsetji Tata inspired their sons with their own missionary zeal. Asoka sent one of his sons to Ceylon to spread Buddhism. Jamsetji Tata's sons (and his inner circle whom he inspired) accomplished his three great schemes after his death: India's first steel plant, its first major hydroelectric project and India's first science research university.

### BABA AMTE: A LIFE OF LOVE

In the 1930s, a Singer sports car carrying a young man was racing to college. When the car stopped and the young man stepped out, one could see a panther's skin spread on the seat. Baba Amte was the son of a rich landlord.

In the following years, Baba Amte became a practising lawyer, gaining acquittals for criminals who paid him handsomely for 'just mumbling a few legalistic words'. As time went by, what Mathew Arnold calls 'a divine dissatisfaction' grew within him. Initially, it showed itself in the form of rebellion against respectability and his way of life—he sported a beard, grew his hair, went barefoot, and neglected the affairs of his father's estate. Although a high-class Brahmin by birth, Baba Amte started associating with untouchables. He would even eat with them at their functions, for which he may not even have been invited. He was deeply distressed that untouchables on his own estate were not allowed to draw water from a nearby well but had to fetch it from one far away. One day he opened the well to the untouchables, despite bitter opposition from his own family.

He says, 'There is a certain callousness in families like mine. They put up strong barriers so as to not see the misery in the world outside and I rebelled against it. I, who had never planted a single seed in the estate, was expected to enjoy the comfort of a beautiful farmhouse, while those who had toiled there all their lives had only the meanest levels.'

His dissatisfaction and yearning for something deeper in life drove him to study at Rabindranath Tagore's Visva-Bharati University, Santiniketan, for three months. The university, known for its unconventional approach to teaching, encouraged people to develop in their own way so they find fulfilment. There, he matured intellectually, learning from Tagore how to appreciate the simple beauty of the universe, and developed a consciousness of God.

Thus he evolved his own standard of conduct and view of society. He pondered over the compassion that he had seen in his mother's eyes and the natural joyfulness he had observed

BABA AMTE

in the Madia Gond tribe of his area. He thought of the lonely courage of Jesus. He ruminated over the poetry and philosophy of Tagore, particularly *Ekla Chalo Re* (walk alone).

On his return home, Baba Amte organized a union of those who collected night soil, the scavengers. When they called for higher wages, he was also the vice-chairman of the municipality for which they worked. The municipality lacked funds and he had to refuse their demands. The strikers charged that he was unsympathetic to their situation because he had never collected a pan of night soil on his head ('imagine our plight during the monsoon,' they pleaded). They challenged him to do the job and then reconsider the decision. Amte accepted the challenge and was assigned forty latrines. Daily, he collected the steel pans of excrement from outhouses and carried them on his head to the disposal site. It was revolting and sickening labour and it affected him profoundly. For one, the experience deepened his regard for and commitment to the outcastes of life. The scavengers received their raise.

However, an incident occurred while Amte was carrying the night soil, an event that would change his life. It was a rainy night and a maggot-ridden leper was lying in the rain, emitting a foul smell. Despite his daily association with human waste, Amte was revolted. He grabbed some mats lying nearby and covered the wretch and hurried away. 'Would I,' he later thought in horror, 'have run away like that if it had been my wife or child?' For months, the shame of cowardice dogged him. He struggled with his conscience and expressed his innermost thoughts, in the words of a poet, Carlos Rodriguez:

I sought my soul, my soul I could not see,
I sought my God, my God eluded me,
I sought my brother, I found all three.

Like G.K. Chesterton, he wondered how man could find sublime inspiration in the ruins of old temples and churches but none when he saw the ruin of a fellow human being. 'I took up leprosy work not to help anyone,' Amte later claimed, 'but to overcome that fear in my life. That it did good to others was a by-product.'

At the age of thirty-two, he developed a fondness for a young lady, Sadhana Guleshastri. He was moved when he saw her quietly helping an old servant hang clothes to dry. Later he recalled, 'I felt married at that moment.' Soon he married Sadhana, or Sadhana Tai as she later came to be known.

After his wedding, he bought a small piece of land, and with his wife, began looking after victims of leprosy. Besides medical treatment, he also wanted to give them purpose and dignity. When he found his skills inadequate to treat them medically, he took a short course at the Calcutta School of Tropical Medicine. In 1949, he established the Maharogi Seva Samiti (Leprosy Relief Society) as a public trust.

When Baba Amte asked the government for land, he was given twenty hectares of disused land with a quarry and scrub forest that was infested with snakes and scorpions. These areas were once hunting estates of British governors. 'An outcast land for an outcast people,' he called it. However, he optimistically named it 'Anandvan' (Forest of Bliss). He started work with six lepers and a lame cow, with the idea of engaging them in farming. But people were afraid to buy the produce because it was farmed by lepers.

Amte was acutely aware that leprosy not only harms the body but also inflicts deep wounds on the mind. It destroys the personality. 'A man can live without fingers, but he cannot live without his self-respect,' Baba Amte would say, adding that 'charity destroys, work builds up a person'. He helped the lepers to become self-dependent, either through farming or by training them in crafts. He also started a school, a college, and a home for the aged called 'Wisdom Bank'. He encouraged healthy retired people to spend their remaining years in this home. Several retired technocrats, government servants, schoolteachers, and army personnel joined him in his work.

For decades, Baba Amte continued his work. Initially, his wife and his two sons, Vikas and Prakash, were his only helping hands. Many of the so-called respectable people avoided him because of the work that he did. At one point, he joked, 'I am more isolated than my patients!' Undeterred, he continued his work. In time, others followed.

Though he won a number of prizes for social service, he was like Mother Teresa in that he never worked with the idea that he was contributing to social welfare. He would say:

A man of faith is not necessarily a Hindu, or Muslim or Christian, nor is he spirituality other-worldly. Indeed, science and spirituality are two sides of the same coin. An introspective search for an order within an individual is 'spirituality'. When that search is turned outwards, we call it 'science'. Both spirituality and science are applied to transform the human being.

The life of Jesus Christ inspired Amte considerably. He realized that when lepers were expelled from their families and society and no one dared come near them, Jesus Christ was full of compassion for them. It was He who healed them with his touch. At the end of an article 'Karunecha Kalam' (the Voice of Compassion) in *The Bloom* (October–December 1992), he addresses the crucified Jesus Christ: 'The cross on which you spent your last breath has become to me not a sign that your service has come to an end. I see it as the sum of all that gives value to our life.' According to Baba Amte, Christ no longer bears the cross, but a plough in the form of a cross. The plough is used to prepare fields for the harvest. In the cross he sees the power that can change the hearts of men; it is a power that can transform the *love of life* into a *life of love* and thus prepare one for a happy and fulfilling future. As Amte said, 'When I come across a leprosy patient, foul-smelling, ulcerous, I can see the imprint of His kiss on the forehead—that is all I see, just His lips, His kiss.'

People who serve humanity like Mother Teresa and Baba Amte have a vision for India. Baba Amte's vision was an India where people give top priority to welfare activities, not power and wealth, and where the objective will be to attend to everyone's needs, rather than a few persons' greed. He envisioned a country where the rich and powerful will have no privileges and the weak and the suffering will be cared for;

a country where people will regard one another as brothers and sisters, and share each other's joys and sorrows. He once undertook a march from Kanyakumari to Kashmir with the slogan, 'Knit India'.

Even at an advanced age, Baba Amte led an active life. In his late eighties, he joined the Narmada Bachao Andolan, a movement against the building of a dam on the great Narmada River. And almost till the last day of his life, although incapacitated by a spine problem, he would be wheeled out of his house every day to hear the sound of the birds at daybreak and to rejoice in the trees around him. Sadhanatai attended to all his needs. His son Vikas once said: 'Father is a perfectionist, obstinate, stubborn and can be very difficult. She is the only one who can deal with him. They are both fused.'

Baba Amte has been the recipient of several international awards, including the Templeton Award and the Magsaysay Award. But perhaps his greatest reward is the divine grace that was instrumental in building his work. This grace has also worked through both his children and other people, who have unhesitatingly come forward to serve his two institutions: one for lepers and another for tribals.

## PRAKASH AMTE: IN HIS FATHER'S FOOTSTEPS

During my eighteen years as director of the Sir Dorabji Tata Trust, many interesting people walked into my office, including a few celebrities. One day, an unassuming couple—Dr Prakash Amte and his wife, Mandakini—came in.

PRAKASH AMTE IN HIS ANIMAL ORPHANAGE

I had vaguely heard of their work with tribals in forest areas and had thought Prakash ran a kind of branch of his father's work with lepers.

He told me that in the vast forest in which he worked, tribals suffered from myriad diseases and also sustained serious injuries from their encounters with wild animals. Apart from the one hospital, the tribals had nowhere to turn to. Malnutrition had made even young tribal people look much older than they were. Prakash was studying for his MD when he first came into contact with the tribals.

In fact, Baba Amte had taken his sons on a picnic to the nearby tribal area of Hemal Kasa, some time after they had passed their college exams. The condition of the tribals moved his younger son, Prakash, and he decided to help them. They asked the government for land in 1971, but it was only in 1974 that the government gave them the land. 'I am grateful to the government,' Prakash says. 'Had they given it to me earlier, I would not have met my wife—an anaesthetist.' His wife, though used to city life, readily joined him in the forest.

Prakash decided that he wanted to go beyond assisting lepers and provide medical treatment to the tribals. The couple showed me gory photos of injuries inflicted by wild animals: a bear on its two rear feet, clawing out the skull of a tribal man.

To avert malnutrition, the couple encouraged the tribals to grow their own vegetables. Till then, they had been unable to do this; their diet consisted of all sorts of animals—dogs, cats, hens, birds, monkeys—and they would often dry and preserve the meat to eat later. At first, it was very difficult for the Amtes to even communicate because the Madia Gond tribe does not have an extensive vocabulary. Prakash's wife, Mandakini, had a graduate diploma in anaesthetics and was a lecturer at a government ayurvedic college. She resigned her post and joined Prakash in 1974. He constructed a small hut for themselves and a bigger one for the patients. There, sometimes under candlelight, the multiple injuries inflicted by a wild boar would be stitched up.

Fortune smiled on them when a representative of Swiss Aid Abroad came to meet them. Moved by the conditions in which work was being done, the organization offered funding houses, a hospital, a godown, as well as borewells and a diesel engine. In later years, many organizations like Oxfam and Sir Dorabji Tata Trust followed suit. Education was another need, so they started a school which is now attended by some 500 tribal students. The hospital has a turnover of 40,000 patients a year.

So impressed was I by the work of Prakash Amte and Mandakini that I requested them to stay a day longer and meet some of the others at the trust. However, they were unable to stay on since there was no doctor in their area and in case of injuries, the tribals would need instant medical attention. I was touched by the dedication of the couple. Here was I working in an air-conditioned office and this couple was facing the challenges of helping a tribal society.

To work out the possibility of them securing a grant from the trust I was heading, I sent one of our senior programme officers, a lady called Jasmine Pavri, to have a look around Hemal Kasa and the project there. She had an interesting but also potentially frightening experience. One night, she heard such a loud roar outside her window that she could have fallen out of bed in fright! In the morning she spoke to the Amte couple about her experience. They said, 'Oh that is our lion whom we set free at night.' Prakash Amte had an animal home in which he roamed fearlessly at daytime with panthers, the lion and other wild animals!

Prakash had not intended to take on any additional responsibilities, but one day, he found that the tribals had killed two macaques and were carrying them home on a rod. One was a dead female with a baby monkey clinging to her breast; the baby was alive. The sight moved Prakash immensely and he asked the tribals to give him that baby monkey. They did, but rather reluctantly. For the next few days, he bottle-fed the monkey. Soon it forgot its mother and began to regard Prakash as its parent. The activists who were working with him knew little about raising animals, but their affection for animals empowered them to transcend their lack of training; today, they are excellent help. Prakash doesn't call it an 'animal zoo'. He calls it 'the animal orphanage'. The animals are not released into the wild as the leopards, for example, have not been naturally trained to hunt and may not be able to catch their own prey!

Noticing the work that was underway, the tribals' own attitude to animals began to change. The sight of Prakash caring for the animals made them realize that not every wild animal is an enemy. If the forest had to be protected, getting the tribals to defend the wildlife was crucial.

Like his father, Prakash Amte and his wife, Mandakini, were also chosen for the Magsaysay Award.

The happy end to the story is that ten years after I first met him, Prakash's son had become a doctor and had taken over his father's work. This gave Prakash the leverage to travel. The son married a young lady who is also a doctor!

'Baba never made any demand on us to become doctors, but we knew he would like us to be because he was handicapped by being a lawyer,' Prakash said.

'How many doctors are there in the family now?' I asked.

'Seven,' he replied.

All dedicated to social work. All serving humanity.

The eldest son, Vikas, and his wife, are doctors as well. Vikas, an excellent public relations man, is proud of his parents and the two brothers are intimate and fond of each other. Vikas's son and daughter-in-law work for lepers; they are also doctors.

## Abhay Bhang: Dealing with Infant Mortality

In the heart of central India is the forest area of Gadchiroli. At both ends of it are doctors inspired by their fathers' sense of service. At one end is Baba Amte's family, at the other, the Bhang family. Dr Abhay Bhang's father, Thakurdas, had the distinction of winning four gold medals at Nagpur University. When Gandhiji's Quit India Movement was launched, he too went to jail. In 1945, he gained admission to Ohio University to study economics, at a time when not many Indians studied in America. Before going to the United States, he went to meet Gandhiji and got his blessings. Gandhiji spoke just one sentence: 'If you want to study economics, why don't you go to the villages of India instead of USA?' Coming out of Gandhiji's cottage, the gold medallist tore off his university admission letters and travel documents. Within a month, along with some of his college mates, he went to a village near Wardha. There, he tried to understand rural economics and farming. Fifty-five years later, his son, Dr Abhay Bhang said, 'At the age of eighty-three, with the same enthusiasm and joy, my father is still carrying on the activities of Gandhiji all over the country ... The magic was that Gandhiji practised what he preached.'

The son, it is important to note, has followed the father. In his case, he studied medicine. On his very first day in the dissection hall, a colleague pointed to a girl engrossed in a dissection at another table. The friend said to young Abhay, 'Her name is Rani. She is from Chandrapore. Last year, she had topped the merit list, but could not join since she was underage then. This year, since you are number one, you will be competing with her.' However, instead of competing, they came closer to each other. He came from a poor background and she was a millionaire's daughter. However, like Abhay and his father, she wanted to live in a cottage and serve the needy. Perhaps what brought them closer was a shared dream. They both qualified as doctors. After working for a short time in a village, they asked themselves, 'Why isn't enough research done by Indians in India for diseases like malaria and cholera? How can any research be done in a village where there are no laboratories, no hospitals and no facilities to speak of? Can research be done for rural health in a village itself?'

They decided to go to the Johns Hopkins University at Baltimore to learn the methodology of public health research. They returned to India with heaps of useful material to educate the villagers. They soon found that the only way to work in an Indian village was to know their customs, their beliefs, their superstitions, their faith and to live alongside them.

The biggest problem in the village was high infant mortality—as much as 121 per 1000. Abhay and Rani first started collecting statistics. In most cases, the cause of death was pneumonia. It had already been established in Papua New Guinea that the simplest way to diagnose pneumonia in children was to count the number of breaths a child took. If it was fifty or sixty per minute, then it indicated pneumonia. But the village nurses they worked with could not even count beyond twelve! They had to be trained to count till fifty! A simple machine was invented for that. The death rate in cases of pneumonia came down dramatically: from 74 per cent to 25 per cent! It also became possible to administer treatment effectively. The total infant mortality rate was brought down from 121 per 1000, to 30 per 1000. Seventy per cent of the women in the village were illiterate and the hospital did not have doctors; but with the assistance of the local people something new was pioneered: a model for the Indian Council of Medical Research. America gave the couple the tools; India the experience and the opportunity.

Their research was published in the year 1990 in *Lancet*, a medical magazine. At a WHO meeting on researches in respiratory diseases, their paper got the first award.

# PART V

# 9

## Dr A.P.J. Abdul Kalam
### Reaching for the Youth

The single-mindedness with which former President Abdul Kalam seeks to inspire the youth of India to work for the nation is admirable. He started this crusade even before he was elected President of India. I asked him at what point this purpose came into his life. He said he didn't know, and added, 'I want to reach the youth before the flame dies down in them—before twenty. Even if I affect two or three out of every hundred I address, I have done my work.' One has to understand this concern of Kalam's in the larger context of his vision for a new India.

After one of his talks, a ten-year-old girl came up to Kalam for his autograph. 'What is your ambition?' he asked her. 'I want to live in a developed India', she replied without hesitation. Kalam's joint study with Y.S. Rajan, principal advisor to the Confederation of Indian Industries, titled *India 2020: A Vision for the New Millennium*, was sparked by the answer of this young girl. Kalam firmly believed that it is this younger generation that will make the new India. 'The Indian people can rise well above the present poverty and contribute more productively to their country because of their own improved health, education and self esteem.' He and Y.S. Rajan have spelt out what is needed in terms of food, agriculture processing; biological wealth, health care, etc., by AD 2020.

Kalam's secretary, P.M. Nair, recalling his five years at Rashtrapati Bhavan wrote in his book *The Kalam Effect:*

> Kalam's faith in the youth and his rapport with them have become legendary. He knew that they were the future of the nation and that moulding them properly was the only way the nation would move forward. Not a day passed when he did not find an hour or two to spend with youngsters, hundreds of them, telling them how the future of the nation depended on their honesty, purposefulness and single-minded devotion to achieve the 'mission'—another favourite word—before them. It is unbelievable how he fired their imagination and galvanized them into such a powerful force.

Kalam wrote *Ignited Minds—Unleashing the Power Within India* because he felt the youth are a powerful resource for transforming a 'developing India' to a 'developed India'. It was important to write such a book because any purpose has to be developed, simplified, and expressed in order for it to be comprehended by all.

After he completed his tenure at the Defence Research and Development Organization as scientific advisor to the government, people were curious to know what Kalam's next move would be. At a press conference he announced that he

Dr A.P.J. Abdul Kalam

would shift to Anna University in Chennai, to teach and inspire young people to do something worthwhile for India. Very soon invitation after invitation poured in. In the next few months, he addressed some 100,000 youths. By May 2002, the first feelers came for presidentship of India and he was elected in July. This office gave Kalam and his ideas a wider exposure, and the number of young people he interacted with in the five years of office, reached a million.

Many were disappointed that he was not put up for re-election as President; but he remained unfazed. His purpose is clear: to make India a developed nation. And he continues to work for his mission.

# PART VI

# 10

## PATHWAYS TO A PURPOSE

Wherever God puts us he has something definite just for us to do. There is something He specially created you to do ... Every time we find ourselves in the presence of a need for an opportunity for helpfulness, we may well stop and ask if God has brought us to the point for this very thing. To realize this gives all our commonest life a sacredness that should make us reverent. We are continually serving our King.

J.R. MILLER, *In Green Pastures*

### AVENUES AND IMPEDIMENTS

Purpose does not necessarily descend from heaven. It is the product of one's own search, the seeking of a journey of the spirit, and a desire to let go and let God show you the direction. Being honest with oneself brings peace of heart and also heightens one's credibility where others are concerned. The right choice, taken boldly, has an uplifting quality. Each decision taken in pursuit of a selfless purpose strengthens one's conviction; compromise weakens it. It is through small compromises that the central purpose of our lives seeps out.

Purpose gives a deeper meaning to life and makes it fulfilling. Each one's life is different; hence, each one has to search for it in a distinctive way. The prime condition is reaching beyond oneself. The first question to ask is, 'Am I divided from anyone by hate, anger or competitiveness?' A friend of mine in MRA once said, 'You are as far away from God as you are from the person you are most divided from.' When the door of the heart is opened wide, these doubts and fears find a way out and a fresh breeze of purpose blows through it. The path to a specific noble purpose may begin with compassion, be it for human beings, animals and birds, or the environment. The question to ask is: 'Is someone or the world outside of me the centre of my life or am I at the centre of my own life?'

Donald Nicholl writes in *The Beatitude of Truth*: 'Nothing is more apt than generous alms-giving to cure a person of spiritual aridity and sterility. And, unless a man is stretching his hand to give to the needy, it is in vain for him to stretch his hands to God in search of forgiveness of sins.'

If your search for a purpose is with yourself in the centre, you may run around in circles for a long time. But if it is focused on other people or a cause beneficial to your fellowmen, you may find your own destiny sooner. A friend of mine, Noshir Dadrawala, is executive head of the Centre for the Advancement of Philanthropy. For over twenty years, he has been advising charities on law and tax, and helping them with their queries. 'It has brought me joy that I can help other people in my job and

am so grateful for the opportunity to do so. One must fin[d]
in one's purpose in life.' It is so true. You may have obstac[les]
along the way but the purpose will hold you.

God does have a plan for you and you have a part to play in it.
I visited an old relative in hospital. He exclaimed, 'I am blessed
you have come!' In bringing joy to others by simple acts you find
a purpose: 'What you do for one of these, you also do for me.'
An ego-centred purpose is only ambition. An outward purpose
has an organic character of its own; it grows. We are meant to
live for each other. Our mental and spiritual lives are empty if
people don't enter our lives. In giving we receive.

As mentioned earlier, compassion is often the trigger for
many a noble action. It is compassion that stirred Vinoba Bhave
when he saw the abject poverty of the landless. Compassion
inspired the man who brought about India's Green Revolution,
Dr Swaminathan. It is what inspired Jamsetji Tata to establish
a school for training in silk-making. Compassion releases our
thoughts for the welfare of others, and in so doing, we fulfil
our own destiny.

The next question is: 'What am I ready to give to it?' It
depends on what is nearest to one's heart. Usually, one hears
whispers of a kind (as the chapter on Mother Teresa shows).
They indicate where our heart lies. Sometimes, the challenge
may be frightening and it may be worth talking over with a
trusted friend. Those who give of themselves selflessly are ready
to give of their time, their money, and eventually their entire
selves. 'Am I ready to do that?'

I may say that I discovered my purpose I learnt about the work of the MRA. easure my life against absolute moral ...esty, purity, love and unselfishness, and to ...ine myself to listen to my inner voice. Once my life began to set itself right, the door opened, I found a faith in God, and over the years, my writing became more purposeful. My inner voice not only corrects me through life experiences but directs the course of my life itself.

Purpose once found, needs to be sustained. Different people find it in different ways. For Mother Teresa it was her link with God. She said she was too busy during the course of the whole day to say prayers except in the early mornings and late at night. But throughout the day she would say small prayers like, 'I love you, I trust you, I believe in you, I need you.' She advised, 'Talk to God naturally as a friend.' To discipline oneself in this way, some time for quiet contemplation is needed, some spiritual reading to condition the mind. Reading inspirational books also helps to keep one focussed. It is most important to be alone with oneself and reaffirm one's goals and purposes. This can be done best before the rush of the day or at bedtime. Reaffirmation helps to sustain one's purpose and make life more rich and meaningful.

One needs to develop the insight to recognize that what we are doing is not just for ourselves. If we are not in the centre of it all, success or failure becomes unimportant. When you feel that God has beckoned you, the ego is not involved. Alan Paton wrote in *An Instrument of Thy Peace*:

If our cause is not the highest cause, if it is a nation or a party or a movement or a church, if it is this with which we identify ourselves, then the defeat of our cause is the defeat of ourselves. But if we believe that God is the ground of our being, we can accept defeat because, in a sense, we cannot be defeated.

If you were pursuing a purpose which, for reasons of energy, ill-health or age, you are unable to take on or complete, you can rest in the wisdom of Solzhenitsyn's prayer:

You will enable me to go on doing
As much as needs to be done.
And in so far as I cannot manage it
That means you've allotted the task to others.

I have found that sincerity of purpose and obedience to the inner voice are the two key elements of spiritual growth. Listening to inspirational music and reading books that are inspiring, help sustain one's purpose. A suitable book can awaken our mind and heart to God. Once we feel His loving presence, we may drift away from the book into our own thoughts.

Vinoba Bhave and Mother Teresa attained their purpose because of their trust in God. The importance of faith in God and one's cause is vital for a worthy endeavour. For example, Martin Luther King said, 'If every Negro in the United States turns to violence, I will choose to be the lone voice preaching this is the wrong way.' This kind of conviction does not come lightly, especially when you have been repeatedly attacked. He finally succumbed to the bullet of his assassin, but his sacrifice enabled President Lyndon Johnson to initiate reforms that were now being supported by white public opinion. King paved the way for a Black American to be elected president, forty-two years after his martyrdom.

Sometimes when pursuing a purpose, one may be derailed by temptations. Kishore Rao was a senior official with a textile firm in south India. He left it because of his inner calling to work in the field of philanthropy. He joined Action Aid to start with, and then left it when he decided to establish a hospice for terminally ill cancer patients—the first of its kind in Bangalore. He worked hard and secured land for the project, and also started a separate trust for it. Just then he received an attractive offer from a multinational company asking him to base himself in Singapore and do their philanthropic work for the whole of South-East Asia. He consulted me as a friend. I asked him if it was possible that he create the hospice in India and also work for the multinational in Singapore. He replied that the position was rewarding enough to finance his fortnightly flight to Bangalore so that he could supervise the work. It was obvious that he was very tempted by the offer. I told him, 'Kishore, at the end of your life, when you look back and you feel you haven't done the one thing God put in your hands, how would you feel?' He heard me out and confessed that he was very confused. I realized it would need more than my words to help him decide. I gave him a copy of Henry Drummond's *The Greatest Thing in the World*, which has a chapter on his sermon on 'How to Know the Will of God'.

I met Kishore a month later. He thanked saying, 'I was confused when I came to you; you helped me find clarity.' He had refused the multinational offer.

Henry Drummond makes some pertinent points about knowing God's Will. According to him, it is important to believe that:

(a) God has a Plan for every human life: a private Will for each person and a universal Will expressed in the Ten Commandments and the beatitude in the Sermon on the Mount.

(b) There is God's Will for a career, as well as for character.

(c) It requires a well-kept life to know the Will of God. The instruments to find it are: Reason; Experience; Circumstance (God closes all paths till there is only one way out); and Advice of others.

But the greatest is Obedience—'it is the organ of spiritual knowledge'. An obedient will is a submissive will to a higher power: 'If any man is willing to obey he shall know.'

Another requirement is patience. Waiting is one of the greatest spiritual qualities, something that is often not recognized. God gives in his own time and our job is to be fit instruments when the time comes. One needs to be patient with oneself. Only if you are very lucky will you know in a flash, like Schweitzer did, what you must do. But how many of us have the persistence to devote seven years of our lives to equip ourselves for it? You will not be presented with an entire plan. But if you are patient, the next step will be clear to you.

Whenever God wants to use us as an instrument to do good, impediments can arise from within ourselves or from outside. The major enemies within are doubt and fear. Sometimes, it is fear of being laughed at. Or, it could be other temptations like vanity, sex, money or liquor, things which prevent us from our pursuit of an objective. It is for this reason that we need to examine our lives daily, where we spend our time and our energies. St. Paul would write to his followers about his mission: 'This one thing I do.' And this was to make men realize 'the depth, the width and the breadth of God's love'.

Vanity and desire for self-promotion can lead one to wrong decisions. Either one allows himself to be driven by a cause or one twists the cause to promote one's own interests. Instances of the latter are 'great' dictators like Napoleon and Hitler. It is necessary to sincerely examine oneself and one's motive afresh each day.

Another great impediment is when those closest to us make our lives difficult. Many have experienced it. Although they may not mean to harm us, they often end up making things very difficult.

Lack of self-esteem can also be a limiting factor. Then, the question arises, 'Suppose I fail if I undertake this project? Then people will laugh at me!' The total personality of a man makes a leader. If a leader is honest with himself, he radiates credibility to others. Right conduct has its own uplifting quality. Each decision taken in pursuit of a selfless purpose strengthens one's conviction; compromises only weaken it.

Sheer frustration can also be an impediment to the fulfilment of a purpose. From my personal experience I have seen that even after one has set a central purpose for oneself, especially if it concerns starting an institution, it may be advisable to once again seek divine approval, to reaffirm whether one is to continue with it.

Considering all these factors, it is obvious that the biggest impediments to a noble purpose are bitterness, hate and unbridled ambition for one's own self. The strongest impetus for a noble purpose is love, as demonstrated by the lives of the many personages covered in this book.

For political purposes, people use the weapon of hate and bitterness. Even Gandhi could have nursed bitterness on being thrown out of the train in South Africa. Instead, he forged a strategy based on love and non-violence that would benefit thousands in his own country. If you want to dedicate your life to a noble purpose, the great lives mentioned in this book may inspire you.

In due course, purpose can shift as one moves through life. Jamsetji Tata moved from ambition for himself to a noble purpose for his people. St Augustine moved from a dissolute life to a dedicated one. He knew that his mother prayed for him. He, in turn, would to pray to God, 'Lord make me pure; but not yet.' There is a time for change in each person and one cannot bring it forward. At the right moment St Augustine found God in his life. He then said, 'You made us for Yourself and our hearts are restless until they find their rest in Thee.'

111

From a self-centred life, many have changed gears to a dedicated one, a life in which the heart is given full play.

Refusal to forgive can be a major obstacle in finding a worthy purpose in one's life. Dr Frank N.D. Buchman, as a young church minister, thought his purpose lay in looking after young people. So he took charge of a hospice for young boys and was happy for a while. As the boys grew, so did their appetite for food. His repeated appeals to the six directors of the hospice to allocate more funds for this purpose were turned down. Embittered, he gave up his job. In a short time, his health started to deteriorate and one doctor advised him to go on a foreign tour. He went to the Middle East and the Mediterranean. He was lively on the surface but admitted later, 'The trouble was I took myself with me.' On the tour, he met a friend to whom he said, 'I will never forgive them [the board]'.

One day, when he was in the Lake District of England, he casually dropped in at a little chapel in Keswick. It was sparsely attended and a woman was taking the service. As a minister, he had heard enough church services about the crucifixion of Christ, but this time this preacher depicted the dying Christ as never before: 'I saw the nails in the palms of his hand, I saw the bigger nail on his feet ... the look of sorrow and infinite suffering on his face. I knew I had wounded him but there is a great distance between myself and him and I knew it was my sin of nursing ill-will.'

That very moment he realized that if the members of the board were six erring men, he was the seventh, to have reacted as he did. He went back to his hotel and wrote to the six men

on the board. In his letter, he asked for their forgiveness for
nursing ill-will towards them. He ended his letter with one of
Gandhi's favourite hymns:

When I survey the wondrous Cross
On which the Prince of Glory died,
My richest gain I count but loss
And pour contempt on all my pride.

He confessed that writing the letters 'produced in me a
vibrant feeling as if a strong current of life had suddenly poured
into me, and afterwards, a great spiritual shaking up'. He had
surrendered his bitterness and now felt as if his soul had been
lifted from the anchorage of selfishness. It was the opening of a
new gate in Buchman's life and the beginning of his worldwide
work of Moral Rearmament. Later he enlarged his mission to
help people to change, through applying four absolute moral
standards common to all faiths: honesty, purity, unselfishness
and love. In addition, he introduced for himself and others the
concept of an introspective period of self-examination. Lack of
forgiveness makes you a prisoner of your past. To forgive opens
doors to future opportunities.

We are dependent on people's opinions far more than we
are willing to admit. Perhaps no one had greater courage to go
against the tide of public opinion than President Anwar Sadat
of Egypt. Israel was the sworn opponent of the Arab world. It
had already fought two wars. In this tumultuous situation, Sadat
had the magnanimity to realize that this was a fruitless path. He
had the courage not to let public opinion be an impediment to

his major purpose, which was to bring peace and prosperity to his people, rather than wage a war of revenge. Not to let others influence one's mission was expressed beautifully by Nobel Prize Winner (1911) Rabindranath Tagore in his poem, 'Ekla chalo re', that if nobody follows you, 'walk alone', a thought Sadat adhered to in his own way.

Sadat confessed to Shimon Peres, who was then Israel's foreign minister (he would later become the prime minister and president of Israel), that he [Sadat] kept moving from one cabin to another, from one palace to another, because he was in search of solitude. It was this solitary engagement with the self that freed him from daily routine and permitted him to quietly meditate. This inclination to be alone with his thoughts, to be in command of his time, to have the leisure to prefer a tree to a desk, and a flower to a file, transformed him into the model leader so often described in books but so rarely found in life.

The biography of Sadat as a president is a story of several great decisions: the liberalization of Egypt in the wake of Nasser's rule, the expulsion of the Russians from Egypt, the October war in 1973, the historical trip to Jerusalem. A great leader, uncompromising in his struggle for peace, Sadat remained true to his purpose till his assassination.

## FINDING ONE'S PURPOSE: ONE STEP AT A TIME

At a time of great personal conflict about whether to be converted from the Protestant to the Catholic denomination of the Church, Cardinal Newman found himself trapped in an epidemic in Italy. People around him were dying like flies, but by a miracle he recovered. In *Light from Many Lamps*, editor Lillian Eichler Watson writes about Newman:

> All at once he saw meaning and purpose in the pattern of his suffering. He had been struck down by the hand of Providence, and by that very hand, had been raised up again! He felt sure he had been saved for a purpose, that God had work for him to do. He was filled with love and gratitude, and with a great humility.

Before his ship left the shores of Italy, Cardinal Newman wrote *Lead Kindly Light*, one of the most beautiful hymns ever written. So greatly influenced by this hymn was Mahatma Gandhi, that one of his biographers, Vincent Sheean, used it as the title of his book on Gandhi. Newman's hymn begins:

> Lead, kindly Light, amid the encircling gloom,
> Lead thou me on;
> The night is dark, and I am far from home;
> Lead thou me on.
> Keep thou my feet; I do not ask to see
> The distant scene; one step enough for me.

The operative words are 'I do not ask to see/ The distant scene; one step enough for me'. As we take one step after another in the Kindly Light, without impatience, but with love for others and faith in a Divine Being and ourselves, the plan unfolds. We need to believe that,

His purposes will ripen fast
Unfolding every hour;
The bud may have a bitter taste,
But sweet will be the flower.

You will never find a higher purpose until you look beyond yourself to the needs of other people.